Psalms
(20-29)

Bookby**Book**

ISBN No: 1-905975-04-X

Published by Biblical Frameworks Limited

Reg. Office: St Paul's Church, Robert Adam Street, London W10 3HW

Cover design, typesetting and production management by Verité CM Ltd, Worthing, West Sussex UK +44 (0) 1903 241975

Illustrations by Richard Thomas

Printed in England

Biblical Frameworks is registered in England No: 5712581

BIBLE STUDY 1: PSALM 20

This psalm lets us see the prayer of the ancient Church to the Father. The Church prays for her Redeemer, the Messiah, to be made victorious.

1. Ancient Israel prays this psalm about the Promised Messiah. Who does she call on to help Christ's victory? How does this help us in our own prayer lives? Who can we pray directly to and how? Look at Jesus' teaching on this in Matthew 6:6-9.

2. When is the time of "distress" talked about in verse 1?

3. What is the sacrifice and burnt offering mentioned in verse 3? There were thousands of animal sacrifices that were made on behalf of the ancient Church. They are often spoken of in the Scriptures. Why then does the psalm focus on the sacrifice from this particular Person? Why is it so special?

4. Why would the Church pray verse 4? What are the desires of the Messiah's heart, and what are His plans? (See, for example, Isaiah 65:17-25; Hebrews 12:1-2, 25-29; or Romans 8:18-25.)

5. According to this psalm, as Christians, what should make us joyful (verse 5)? How does this ensure that we can be joyful whatever our circumstances?

6. What are banners for? (verse 6) How should the banners of the Church be identified? How can this be the case in the way we live our lives?

7. In verses 7 & 8, how does the gospel turn all worldly perspectives and expectations upside-down? How can knowing this help us when we are ridiculed for what we believe?

8. What does this psalm show us about how closely Christ is connected to us, His Church, through His sufferings? As Christians, should we be able to look on the Cross without feeling?

Psalm 22: The psalm of the Cross

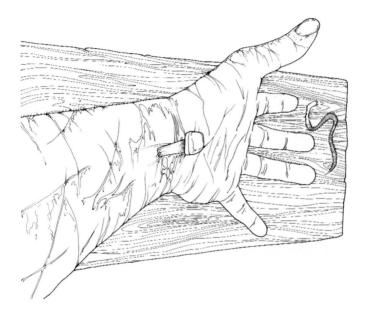

"I am a worm and not a man..."

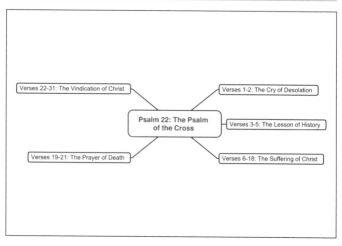

Verses 22-31: The Vindication of Christ

Verses 1-2: The Cry of Desolation

Psalm 22: The Psalm of the Cross

Verses 3-5: The Lesson of History

Verses 19-21: The Prayer of Death

Verses 6-18: The Suffering of Christ

Key Truth: This psalm gives us an insight into the very thoughts and feelings of the Christ as He hung dying on the Cross.

In C. H. Spurgeon's "Treasury of David", he says of this psalm, "This is beyond all others THE PSALM OF THE CROSS. It may have been repeated word by word by our Lord when hanging on the tree... It is the photograph of our Lord's saddest hours, the record of His dying words... Before us we have a description both of the darkness and the glory of the Cross, the sufferings of Christ and the glory that shall follow. Oh for grace to draw near and see this great sight! We should read reverently, putting off our shoes from off our feet, as Moses did at the burning bush, for if there be holy ground anywhere in Scripture it is in this psalm."

This psalm describes the sufferings of Jesus so accurately that it has been called *'history written in advance.'*

1. The cry of desolation – verses 1-2

In Matthew 27:46 Jesus cried out verse 1 of Psalm 22, allowing us to see that David's sombre prediction of His suffering had come true. The depth of desolation and darkness in His cry was explained and dissected by David so long before.

"This word 'My God' takes in more than all the philosophers in the world could draw out of it" – Alexander Wedderburn, 1701. We are faced here with the inner turmoil of the divine life on the Cross.

How could the Eternal Son, the LORD's Christ, utter such words? How could the Father abandon the Son? Surely, this would be the end of the Living God, the God who is Father, Son and Holy Spirit.

Of course, the temptation is to explain these words away, to minimise their significance. Yet, when we meditate on the Cross of Christ we *must* face it in all its terror and darkness if we are to appreciate what was happening for our salvation.

2 Corinthians 5:21 – "God made Him who had no sin to *be* sin for us, so that in him we might become the righteousness of God."

When Jesus hung on the Cross suffering the anger of God against sin, the impossible happened: the Father turned His face away from the Son, the LORD turned away from His Messiah. We can never imagine the utter desolation that Jesus experienced at that time. He had known the overwhelming love of the Father from everlasting... *until* those hours. Never before and never since has there been anything but infinite love between the Father and the Son. But at that time the uninterrupted life of the Living God was disrupted as the condemnation of our sin was answered within the life of God.

When we read these words we are ushered into the deepest and most terrible suffering that there ever has been and ever will be.

Whatever desolation we experience we can enter into this psalm and find expression for it. Our Mediator understands where we are, no matter how deep our suffering.

2. The lesson of history – verses 3-5

When He became one of us through the Virgin Mary, the Lord entered into the whole of what it means to be an earthly human. He learned His theology as we learn theology, through the Scriptures. When we are given a brief glimpse of His childhood in Luke 2:41-52 we see a boy completely enthralled by the Hebrew Scriptures. In the Scriptures He found His own identity and work described in great detail.

In these verses of Psalm 22 we see that as He hung on the Cross, the Messiah recalled to mind the lives of the saints in the Scriptures. He remembered how previous generations of believers had trusted in the Living God. He remembered that every single one had received salvation. They were not disappointed in their faith.

This was the foundation truth that He had to rest upon at that time. When He hung on the Cross in God-forsaken agony, He knew that He could trust Himself completely to His Father's will. Through the Scriptures, history had taught Him the lessons He needed to sustain Him in the darkest hour.

3. The suffering of Christ – verses 6-18

When we read this section of the psalm we are amazed at the accuracy of David's prophecy. It is as if he had seen the crucifixion with his own eyes. Here the profound nature of prophecy is revealed. The vague and ambiguous ramblings of Nostradamus are shown up for what they are by the clarity, accuracy and specificity of the great prophet David.

Yet, nothing can prepare us for the words of verse 6 – "I am a worm and not a man..." In His suffering Jesus felt so isolated, so cut off from both human and divine life that He felt as if He had lost His humanity. He felt as if He were nothing more than a helpless creature, trodden underfoot. Christ the Lord, the One through Whom and for Whom everything was created, the One infinitely above the greatest angel, was brought so low, suffering so deeply, that His own humanity seemed lost to Him.

Notice, verses 7-8, that it is the rejection of the people that provokes such dark thoughts in Him. The crowds mocked and insulted Him, shaking their heads in scorn at the mess He was in. He wanted human sympathy and friendship at that time. He longed for the words of His Eternal Father telling Him that He was loved… and that was the very focus of the insults. Why didn't the Lord deliver Him from this cursed, God-forsaken death?

Yet, verses 9-11, His trust is unshaken. He remembers how He has trusted in His Father even when He was in His mother's womb. When He was helpless then He trusted. When there is no one to help, He will still trust His God.

He feels as if He were surrounded by wild animals (v12-13). The people hate Him and only want to destroy Him. It is this that causes Him such distress. He is dying to save the world even when the world hates Him. His whole body feels broken in His suffering – v14-15.

Verse 16 is a wonderful prophecy of the crucifixion of the Messiah – "they have pierced my hands and feet." *Nothing like that ever happened to David, yet it precisely described the way Jesus was killed.*

In v17 we are able to look through the eyes of the Messiah on the Cross. We are taken so deeply into the most terrible event there will ever be. What can He see? The bones of His own body showing through His skin… and the people staring at Him, gloating over Him.

Just as David prophesied, verse 18, Jesus' clothes were divided up among the soldiers – John 19:23-24.

4.   The prayer of death – verses 19-21

In such grief, Jesus remains the Man of Faith. He still trusts His Father. He has prepared Himself throughout His life for this time. He must have read this psalm, and all the other prophecies of His death so many times throughout His life. Now, at the end He remains faithful and entrusts His life to His Father.

As He dies He asks His Father to deliver His life from death. In Luke 23:46 we see how Jesus did this.

5. The vindication of Christ – verses 22-31

In Hebrews 12:2 we are told that Jesus "for the joy set before Him endured the cross, scorning its shame". He could get through the pain and humiliation of His crucifixion because He was so focused on the final outcome.

In the final section of this psalm we are shown how the Messiah thought about "the joy set before Him" even in His agony.

It is thoughts of Church life that He looks forward to. It is the fact of His sharing the human life of His Church that fills His mind (see Hebrews 2:10-12). He imagines how wonderful it will be to teach the Church more about His Father and how He will join them in Christian worship. Such thoughts make Him want to lead the praise right away – verse 23. Can it really be true that in the depth of His suffering His heart was lifted in praise to His Father? Yes, and He goes on to explain this.

However forsaken Jesus felt, nevertheless, He knew that His Father did not despise or ignore "the suffering of The Afflicted One." Far from turning away from the Cross, the Father's entire attention was fixed on that suffering. Jesus knew that it was in His suffering that the glory of God was being revealed to the world.

So He imagines Himself at the centre of a "great assembly" of Christian worship, all focused on the Father. As we study the following verses, we see that it isn't just any time of praise... it is the great assembly of Resurrection Morning, when the saints from all over the world and from every period of history will gather around Jesus Christ to worship the Father. In verse 26, He thinks of the way

He will satisfy all poverty and grant immortality to those who seek the Lord. People from every nation will turn to the Lord (verses 27-28), including the rich as well as the poor (v.29). The dead, whose bodies have become dust, will be resurrected to kneel in worship in that great assembly.

In verses 30-31 we see how the Messiah thought ahead to the many generations of people who would come to a knowledge of the Living God because of what He was doing. They would be able to tell the gospel to other future generations (v31). But, how can this be? As Christ looked down from the Cross He could only see the scornful faces of people who hated Him. How could He be so sure that things would turn out so well in the end? The final phrase of the psalm explains – the Lord has done it. This is no human work. The whole human race is simply a spectator of the Cross of Jesus. It is the ultimate work of the Living God to turn us from Christ-hating rebels to Christ-loving members of that great assembly.

Further Questions

1. It has been said that God is most clearly revealed at the Cross. How can this be true at the very time when the Father forsakes the Son?

2. In verse 6, God the Son, the Messiah-Lord feels as though He has lost His humanity. Have we noticed how highly humanity is regarded throughout the Bible? What does this tell us about the agonies of the Cross?

3. Verse 1 is the cry of Jesus at the beginning of His death on the Cross. Look at Psalm 31:5. What might this tell us about the Scriptures between these two verses?

Daily Readings

Sunday: Psalm 22

Monday: Matthew 27:27-61

Tuesday: Philippians 2:1-18

Wednesday: Isaiah chapter 53

Thursday: Ephesians 2:11-22 and Romans 5:1-11

Friday: 1 Corinthians 1:18-2:5

Saturday: Revelation chapter 5

BIBLE STUDY 2: PSALM 22

Have you ever wondered how the Messiah endured those hours of suffering and shame while He hung on the Cross for us? This psalm lets us see what kept Him there and His own thoughts during His darkest moments.

1. We recognise the opening of the psalm as Christ's words on the Cross (Matthew 27:46). What is the significance of this cry? Had the relationship between Father, Son and Holy Spirit ever been shaken before?

2. Why was the Lord's Messiah forsaken? What does this tell us about the seriousness of sin?

3. What would it have meant for Jesus to be facing death and abandoned by His Father? How should this effect our relationship with Jesus Christ through any sufferings that we face?

4. In verses 3-5, Jesus comforts Himself in His agony. What things does He think about to give Him relief? Does this surprise us? What does it tell us about how Christ values us His Christian family?

5. What is it that particularly causes the Messiah so much suffering in verses 6-11? Why? What can we learn from Christ's own response to this about what we can do when there is no-one to help us?

6. How many parallels can we see in verses 14-18 with what happens to Jesus when He dies on the Cross? We could perhaps compare this with an account of the Cross in John 19.

7. From verses 21 to the end, the thoughts of Christ turn from pleas to save Him from death into praising the Father. How could this happen during the agony He was suffering?

8. In this psalm we have looked into the heart of the deepest and most painful sufferings the world has known and ever will know. What lessons have we learnt about what our own responses to suffering should be?

Psalm 23: The psalm of resurrection hope

"Though I walk through the valley of the shadow of death"

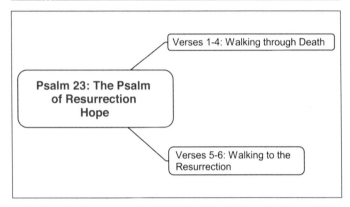

Verses 1-4: Walking through Death

Psalm 23: The Psalm of Resurrection Hope

Verses 5-6: Walking to the Resurrection

Key Truth: The most well known psalm describes the comforting words of the Messiah as He faces His own death on the Cross.

Psalm 23 is the most well known psalm. Many of us learnt it when we were children and its calming words can be found in countless settings throughout the world. Every day thousands of dying people listen as the psalm is read to them. Although the psalm fits within this series of psalms dealing with the death, resurrection and ascension of the Messiah, we find such comfort for ourselves in this psalm.

Jesus, the Good Shepherd, will guide us through the valley of the shadow of death just as His Father gave Him protection from the power of death.

We might well feel emotionally drained after the intense emotion of Psalm 22. However, Psalm 23 must be read as the aftermath of Psalm 22. The Messiah could pray such a prayer of resurrection confidence because of what He was accomplishing on the Cross. By His Death He won the right to share this psalm, His psalm of resurrection hope, with the whole Church of every age.

1. Walking through death – verses 1-4

In Psalm 22 we saw that in His death Jesus had no sympathisers, no friendly faces, no comforters. In fact He was surrounded by mockers, scorners and insulters. He faced death not just alone, but with every one trying to make death even worse for Him.

In Psalm 23 we see how in spite of all this, His confidence in the face of death was not shaken. With His feelings of God-forsakenness and human rejection, nevertheless Christ had absolute confidence in His Father's will and care. [13]

It begins with such famous words – "The Lord is my Shepherd, I shall not want." He acknowledges that with the Father as His Shepherd He needs nothing else. In a sense the rest of the psalm is simply an explanation of this.

The kind of care that a shepherd gave to his sheep is explained by David in 1 Samuel 17:34-35 – "When a lion or a bear came and carried off a sheep from the flock, I went after it, struck it and rescued the sheep from its mouth. When it turned on me, I seized it by its hair, struck it and killed it."

The Lord's Messiah shows us how to depend completely on the Shepherd, particularly as we face death. When He calls us to trust Him as The Good Shepherd (John 10:11-14), we can know that He has shown us what this looks like in His own relationship with His Father.

Throughout Scripture it is the Messiah Himself who is described as the Shepherd of His people. In Genesis 48, when Jacob is about to die, he confesses that Christ has been his Shepherd all through his life. When he blesses Joseph's two sons he says: "May the God before whom my fathers Abraham and Isaac walked, the God who has been

---

[13] People have argued that Psalm 23 is the prayer of Christ, because of the end of verse 6. The Hebrew is literally, "I will return to the house of the LORD forever". None of us have ever been in the house of the LORD, so we can't return to it!

my shepherd all my life to this day, the Angel [14] who has delivered me from all harm may he bless these boys…" [15]. All these Scriptures must have helped Jesus to understand both Himself and His relationship to His Father in His life and death.

Christ knows exactly the kind of care, protection, and encouragement we need from our Shepherd… because He has experienced this need for Himself, as we have seen in Psalm 22. He knows that we need to be spiritually refreshed throughout our lives and in death. He had experienced the joy and refreshment that the Father gave to Him – verse 2. Luke 10:21 shows us an example of this – "At that time Jesus, full of joy through the Holy Spirit…"

The Hebrew for the beginning of verse 3 is literally "He brings my soul back." Back from what? The answer from Psalm 22 must be "from death". Even when He was condemned as a criminal, Christ knew that the Father would not leave Him in the grave. Yes, even *then*, cursed as He hung on the Cross (Deut. 21:23) He knew that the Father would guide Him in paths of righteousness for His Name's sake.

In verse 4 we get to the very heart of the issue. It is not just difficult times that have to be faced – it is passing through death itself. It is not just 'near' to this valley that Christ had to pass. He didn't have a 'near death experience'. He had to pass *right through* the valley of the shadow of death.

Nevertheless, the striking thing about the phrase is the word 'shadow'. With the Lord as Shepherd even death becomes a shadow of what it was. The sting of death is sin (1 Cor. 15:56). To face death with its sting is a truly horrible prospect. For the unbelieving wicked, death is the beginning of an unimaginably terrible eternity in Hell.

The Messiah, as the sinless and innocent One (see Psalm 26), did not have to face death in that hopeless and desperate way. Yes, He had

---

[14] Note: The Angel of the Lord simply means 'The One sent from the Lord'. He is God – see Genesis 16:11-13. He is the God sent from God. He is the Christ, the Son of the Most High.

[15] See also Isaiah 40:10-11

to pass right *through the* valley, but He did not have to fear evil. He could trust His Father even in the terrible circumstances of the Cross. Even though all His feelings told Him that the Father had forsaken Him, that He had to face death completely alone, YET, 'you are with me' (verse 4). Yes, even when He was sin on the Cross bearing the consuming wrath of God against sin, even then He knew that (2 Cor. 5:19) God was in Him reconciling the world to Himself.

If that was true of Christ in His own death, then this psalm can give us tremendous comfort as we face our own journey through the valley. Because of Christ's death and resurrection we need fear no evil in that valley. The Lord takes up this very theme through the prophet Hosea when He speaks of His care for His people. "I will ransom them from the power of the grave; I will redeem them from death. Where, O death, are your plagues? Where, O grave, is your destruction?" (Hosea 13:14).

In Jesus Christ death is emptied of its terror.

Throughout the Bible "the rod of the Lord" stands for His judgement against sin and evil – see Psalm 2:9 and Psalm 89:32. It is a great comfort to know that vengeance and judgement belong to the Lord. Evil and wickedness may seem to have the last word, but the rod of the Lord tells us that justice and goodness and righteousness have the final say. Even though Jesus had to bear the full power of that rod against Him on the Cross, yet it was a great comfort for Him to know the reality of that rod. When He was surrounded by the power of evil, He needed to know that evil would not triumph. He could face death knowing that 'vengeance belongs to the Lord'. He was able to reject Peter's temptation to use the sword because of this – John 18:10-11. He did not call for legions of angels, because He could trust in the final Day of Judgement – Matthew 26:53. He kept silent when false accusations and misleading questions were put to Him – 1 Peter 2:21-25. He did all this because of the comfort He received from the Father's rod and staff.

If we are to face death without fear, we must remember that all injustice will be set right by Him on the Day of Judgement.

2. Walking to the Resurrection – verses 5-6

The language of the psalm changes from verse 5. We are no longer thinking of the Shepherd and His sheep, but a guest arriving at a banquet in the Lord's house. This is the Son going to His Father's mansion. We will see in Psalm 24 (and Psalm 68) just how warm a welcome He would receive in His Father's house!

Christ knew that He would receive this welcome when He *returned* to His Father's house. Even while He is taunted on the Cross, even while (Psalm 22:16) "Dogs have surrounded me; a band of evil men has encircled me, they have pierced my hands and my feet", yet He knew that heaven was waiting for Him. He knew that a table was being prepared for Him.

We know that He had such a great hope because of what He said to the thief who was crucified next to Him. Luke 23:42-43 – "Then he (the criminal) said, 'Jesus, remember me when you come into your kingdom.' Jesus answered him, 'I tell you the truth, *today you will be with me in paradise.*'"

Sometimes Christians talk as if Jesus had to go down to Hell until He was resurrected on Easter Sunday. However, the Bible tells us the very opposite. When He died, quoting Psalm 31:5, He went to paradise to be welcomed by His Father. When He cried out 'It is finished', then it was indeed finished. There was nothing left to do or pay. The full work of atonement was carried out on the Cross by the Messiah, and He did not continue to pay for sin beyond the Cross. There was nothing to prevent Him going to His Father's house. [16] Within three days Jesus would be back from the dead in a

---

[16] Of course, Jesus was in paradise without a body in the time between the Cross and the Resurrection. The glory of the Ascension is that He entered into the Most Holy Place of paradise with His human body – see Hebrews 10:19-21.

resurrection body, showing us the glorious renewed physical future that we have in Him.

In verse 5 Christ celebrates the fact that He is the Messiah, the Anointed One: "You anoint my head with oil."

Throughout the Bible we see that prophets, priests and kings had to be anointed to do their job. In Leviticus 8:12 we see that the most senior priest at the tabernacle had his head anointed with oil to consecrate him to his job. In fact every priest had to be anointed – Exodus 28:41. In 1 Kings 19:16 Elijah the prophet anointed Elisha to be his successor. Whenever a man was set apart to be a king then a priest or prophet anointed his head with oil – 1 Samuel 10:1; 1 Kings 1:39; 2 Kings 9:6.

David's anointing with oil also shows us what this oil was a sign of: "Samuel took the horn of oil and anointed him in the presence of his brothers, and *from that day on* the Spirit of the LORD came upon David in power" 1 Samuel 16:13.

Jesus knew that His Father had anointed Him with the oil of the Spirit. At the beginning of His public ministry He received a special anointing for service – Matthew 3:16-4:1. Notice how the Father gives such a strong affirmation of His love for the Son at that time.

The Messiah is the original and foundational Prophet, Priest and King. All the prophets, priests and kings of the Old Testament were symbolic prophecies of Him. The faithful ones believed this and drew attention to it (David in Psalm 2). The fact that the Messiah Jesus was anointed with the Spirit without measure showed that the Father had unconditional confidence in Him. As He hung on the Cross, Hebrews 9:14 tells us that He offered Himself by the Eternal Spirit to His Father. In other words, He was fulfilling His role as The Anointed Priest even *then* in the darkness and suffering.

This is why His cup overflows and He has such confidence in the goodness and love of His Father for ever and ever. He has shown us how to rejoice in the great blessings that the Father gives to us, no matter what circumstances we find ourselves in.

The oil of the Spirit that was given to Jesus overflows down onto His body, the Church. We too know the presence of the Spirit in all our journey, right through the valley of death.

Ephesians 1:3 – "Praise be to the God and Father of our Lord Jesus Christ, who has blessed us in the heavenly realms with every spiritual blessing in Christ." We can do this knowing that Jesus Christ knew the same joy. He knew that He would return to the house of the Lord, that all the suffering and rejection He was experiencing could not finally separate Him from His Father. Both now as Christ waits with His Father to return to earth and finally when the Father's city will come down out of heaven to earth (Rev. 21:1-4), His home is always and forever 'the Lord's house'.

The resurrection confidence of the psalm continues to comfort thousands of Christians every day. Christ has shown us how to keep our attention fixed on the resurrection future through death, knowing that the Father will never abandon those who trust Him.

Further Questions

1. Why was Jesus' death on the Cross so particularly bad? Wasn't it just like any other cruel death? Haven't other people suffered more than Him?

2. Many of us will read this psalm to people when they are ill or dying. Is it appropriate to offer any explanation of the Messiah as we do this? How might we be able to explain the meaning of the psalm with comfort, love and grace?

3. How does Hosea 13:14 relate to this psalm? Look also at Paul's explanation in 1 Corinthians 15:53-57.

Daily Readings

Sunday: Psalm 23

Monday: Matthew 27:62-28:15

Tuesday: John 10:1-18

Wednesday: 1 Corinthians 15:1-34

Thursday: 1 Corinthians 15:35-58

Friday: Ezekiel chapter 34

Saturday: John 11:1-44

BIBLE STUDY 3: PSALM 23

The words of this psalm offer deep comfort for us all as we face death, because it comforted the Messiah as He faced the ultimate death with certain future hope.

1. Who is the Good Shepherd of the Church? (John 10:11-14)

2. What are verses 2 and 3 describing? What does this mean for us today in practical terms? Can we experience this?

3. Why does Jesus refer to death as just a 'shadow', verse 4? What would be the worst way to face death? How is He so confident as He walks right through it?

4. Why don't we need to fear death? See Hosea 13:14.

5. The Bible constantly assures us that all evil and injustice will be brought to account on Judgement Day. The rod of judgement will destroy the power of evil. How can this knowledge affect the way we think and act? How should it affect our prayers?

6. We have seen that fixing our eyes on the certain future with Christ and the Father helps us face death. How can it be possible to do this when the world around us never mentions it?

7. What relevance does this most-famous psalm have for us? (1 Corinthians 15:20-23)

Psalm 24: The psalm of the ascension

"Lift up your heads, O you gates... that the King of glory may come in"

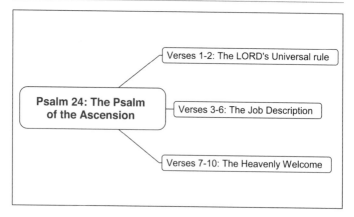

Psalm 24: The Psalm of the Ascension

Verses 1-2: The LORD's Universal rule

Verses 3-6: The Job Description

Verses 7-10: The Heavenly Welcome

Key Truth: In this psalm the Church celebrates the triumphant ascension of her Lord after the victory of the Cross.

It has been thought by some that this psalm was composed and sung when the Ark of the Covenant was lifted up and brought to Jerusalem by King David – 1 Chronicles 15:29-16:3. There is a lot to be said for this, especially when we look back to how Moses reacted whenever the Ark of the Covenant was lifted up during the journeys in the wilderness – Numbers 10:35: "Whenever the ark set out, Moses said, 'Rise up, O LORD! May Your enemies be scattered; may Your foes flee before You.'"

Those words of Moses are expanded into an entire psalm by David, Psalm 68, which describes the ascension of Jesus Christ after His death and resurrection (see Ephesians 4:8-13). This makes it clear that Moses saw the lifting up of the Ark of the Covenant as a symbolic prophecy of the ascension of Christ. Whenever the Ark was lifted up, he looked ahead to the day when Christ would be lifted up to the right hand of His Father in heaven after being brought down so low in His birth, life and death.

So, it might well be that when David also lifted up the Ark and brought it in procession to the earthly Jerusalem, he saw that it was a symbolic prophecy of the day when Christ would be lifted up and led in joyful procession to the right hand of His Father in the heavenly Jerusalem, the City of God. Given the deep prophetic knowledge of David that we saw in Psalm 22, we would expect this psalm to be similar.

However, we are not told exactly when this psalm was written or the circumstances when it was first sung. The one thing that is clear is that it is a psalm prophesying the ascension of Jesus Christ.

Christopher Wordsworth said of *this* psalm that the universe "is Christ's, by creation (John 1:1-2), and it is His by resurrection (Matthew 28:18), and His by His glorious ascension into heaven where He is enthroned King of the world in His human nature."

1. The LORD's universal rule – verses 1-2

The psalm begins with a simple assertion of the LORD's claim over the universe. The world and everything in it all belongs to the LORD. His claim is based on the fact that He made it all. We would think that nobody could ever question the right of the Father, Son and Holy Spirit to rule over their creation. Surely everything must entirely belong to the Living God!

However, as we examine our own experience of the world and our own lives, we *do* question this mighty truth. How *can* everything belong to the LORD when the power of evil is so obviously at work in the world? How can the Trinity rule it all when so much evil seems to rule it? It seems obvious that the LORD does *not* have total control over His world. Surely, the world has rebelled against Him in an alliance with evil spiritual forces; the world runs its *own* way according to its *own* rules.

The LORD's claim on the world needs to be backed up. It needs to be established and demonstrated. Who can do this? Who can take up the LORD's claim, defeat all His enemies and rule the universe?

2. The job description – verses 3-6

The question is posed: who can go into heaven (the hill of the Lord) to rule the universe? Who can defeat all the enemies of God to vindicate the Lord's rule? Who is accepted into the Father's Most Holy presence in order to sit down at His side to govern the world? Who would dare to stand in the presence of God Most High to take up His sovereign rule?

Every sinful human cringes at the thought of such a task. None of us are worthy to even consider such a job. When the world was first created, then perhaps Adam was able to go up the hill of the LORD, which was in the Garden of Eden [17]. But, *now*, who can possibly return to the mountain of God, who can restore the creation to its proper state?

According to verse 4, it is only the One who has clean hands and a pure heart who can do this. Only the One who has never fallen into idol-worship or lies. This is such a great verse for exposing our extreme need of the Messianic-Saviour.

Our hands are *not* clean because they have been involved in all kinds of sin.

Our hearts are *not* pure because they are full of evil desires and selfish motives.

Even if we haven't worshipped the images of pagan gods, we have all fallen into the idol-worship of greed (Colossians 3:5).

However, the One who is free from all sin is the One who will be blessed in the Father's presence – verse 5. Whatever is said or done against that One will be put right from the throne of heaven. The Father will save this One from every enemy and false accusation.

---

[17] See Ezekiel 28 for an example of this truth. In Ezekiel 28:11-15 we see a description of Satan before he fell. He was the guardian cherub in the Garden of Eden. Notice that even in Eden he was able to walk on the holy mount of God. It seems that before the entrance of sin the whole creation, heaven and earth, was joined together and the inhabitants of Eden had access to the mount of God.

Notice that verse 6 is addressed to God in heaven (...seek *Your* face...). However, we also seek "*Him*". We are shown the Church seeking *two things*: the One who can do the job of verses 3-5 and the face of the Father. Those who acknowledge their own need of this One, the One with clean hands and a pure heart, share in His blessing and vindication.

This section of the psalm is followed by "Selah". We are to think about how much we need an answer to this job description and how powerless we are to save ourselves.

3. The heavenly welcome – verses 7-10

The search for '*Him*' is successful. He is found and He is approaching heaven in His ascension, having fought a victorious battle over all the forces of evil. It is good to remember that this psalm cannot be referring to a merely human march up to the earthly temple in the earthly Jerusalem, because the temple didn't even exist during David's reign! The earthly temple was built by his son Solomon.

"The prophet foresees the ascension of Christ and His saints into the kingdom of heaven. He sees the Lord marching at the head of the redeemed world, and conducting them into regions of honour and joy" (James Hervey).

So, verse 7, the procession of the King of Glory approaches the gates of heaven, and those that are with Him call out as they get close: "Get ready to receive the King of Glory; make sure the gates are wide open to welcome Him". The doors are *everlasting* doors (NIV 'ancient') as only the doors of the City of God may be.

This cry is answered with a question from within, verse 8: "who is this King of Glory?" We should not think of this question as implying that heaven is unsure of the legitimacy of Christ. It is rather part of the joyful celebration as He returns in triumph. The saints and angels of heaven love to hear the glory and identity of the Great Lamb announced as He returns in victory.

BookbyBook

The answer is given: "it is the strong and mighty LORD who has defeated all the forces of sin and evil in battle". In His death and resurrection, Jesus stripped the devil of his power and made it possible for sin, death, decay and evil to be driven out of the universe on Judgement Day. There can be no opposition or doubt about His universal rule over creation. All His enemies have been humiliated beneath His feet.

The cry goes up again – "Open the gates, get ready to receive the King of kings and Lord of lords. Welcome Him with great joy and praise!"

Again there is a question, verse 10 – "Who is this King of Glory?" The resounding answer is that He is none other than the Lord Almighty. He has gone out to establish His own claim over the universe. The fact that the question is repeated shows how thrilled the whole of heaven was at the first reply they received! What joy and celebration there must have been when the Lord Messiah, Jesus, ascended to heaven with the power and authority of the whole creation in His hands!

After we have studied this psalm we can see why Paul speaks of the Ascension of Jesus in the way that he does in Ephesians 4:10. In His Ascension, Jesus lays claim over the whole universe having defeated all His enemies at the Cross. All the resources of the cosmos are available to Jesus to use as He wants.

Further Questions

1. How do we celebrate the Ascension each year? Should we send cards to each other, give gifts or hold parties? Should we insist on a public holiday?

2. What understanding of the work of the Messiah must David have had in order to write this psalm? Do you think it had a connection to the lifting up of the Ark of the Covenant, as songs were sung when this happened, for example 1 Chronicles 15:28-16:4? (Compare also Numbers 10:35 with Psalm 68:1)

3. Where else in the Bible do we see the 'hill' or 'mountain' of the Lord? In which locations? This is a fascinating Bible study if you have the time.

Daily Readings

Sunday: Psalm 24

Monday: Acts 1:1-11

Tuesday: Ephesians 4:1-16

Wednesday: Psalm 68

Thursday: Revelation 21:9-27

Friday: Psalm 8

Saturday: Psalm 110

Bookby**Book**

BIBLE STUDY 4: PSALM 24

After the psalms that speak of the death and resurrection of Christ, we now come to a psalm full of praise for the ascension of Christ into heaven.

1. Why are verses 1 and 2 an important start to this psalm? What difference does it make to our prayer life and our praise if we begin them with such an assertion?

2. Where do you think the 'hill of the Lord' is? (eg, Psalm 2:6, or Psalm 3:4)

3. What role is to be fulfilled by the Person who goes there? (See Psalm 103:19 and Psalm 110:2)

4. Who do you think must be speaking this psalm? Why do they need someone with the characteristics of verse 4?

5. Can you identify the two people who bear the name 'Lord' in this psalm? (compare verses 5 and 8) What are their different roles? How do they relate to each other?

6. What is the connection between 'seeking the face of the God of Jacob' and seeking the One who can ascend the hill of the Lord to the God of Jacob? (verse 6)

7. Can you explain the meaning of verse 7? Where are these gates? (see Rev 21:10-25)

8. The psalm is a prophecy of Jesus, the King of glory. What particular battle and victory do you think is celebrated in verse 8?

9. How does Psalm 24 help us understand why it was so important that Jesus ascended into heaven after His resurrection? Why is that so vital for us today? See for example Romans 8:34, Psalm 110:5, Ephesians 1:3, 1 Corinthians 15:20-23.

Psalm 25: In You I trust, o my God

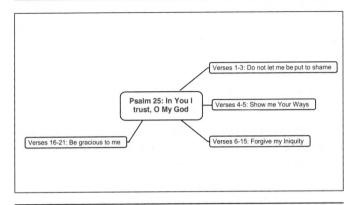

Psalm 25: In You I trust, O My God

Verses 1-3: Do not let me be put to shame

Verses 4-5: Show me Your Ways

Verses 6-15: Forgive my Iniquity

Verses 16-21: Be gracious to me

Key Truth: Here is David's heartfelt response to the future death, resurrection and ascension of the Messiah; a plea for forgiveness and blessing in His relationship with the Lord.

It seems right to see all the psalms we have studied as a set that are connected together. Various writers have speculated that they were originally used together to bring out their meaning. For example, R. H. Ryland in "The psalms Restored to Messiah" (1853) makes the following comment:

"When the Jewish church wished to celebrate the great act of Messiah the High Priest making a sacrifice for the people on the day of atonement, as represented in the twenty-second psalm... we are to suppose... that the series of psalms, from the 20th to the 24th inclusive, was used as a service or office in the public worship of the Jewish church."

In other words, on the Day of Atonement these psalms may have been used to provide the structure for the whole day of worship: beginning with the prayers for the Messiah in Psalm 20, through the confidence that the Messiah would be heard in Psalm 21, the thoughts of the Suffering Messiah on the Cross in Psalm 22, His Resurrection hope in Psalm 23 and His glorious Ascension in Psalm 24.

However, could it be that the series also included Psalm 25 as the conclusion and application of the set?

Psalm 25 seems to follow on naturally from Psalm 24. Psalm 24 ended with Christ going *up* to the City of God and Psalm 25 begins with David lifting *up* his soul to the One he trusts.

Psalm 25 makes such a fitting conclusion to the spiritually exhilarating journey we have made through these psalms. Having joined myself to the Messiah in His battle, I have watched in awe as He hung on the Cross, been filled with hope by His Resurrection, and overwhelmed with joy in the Ascension. Now, I look *up* to the glorified and ascended Messiah and trust in Him with all my heart.

1. Do not let me be put to shame – verses 1-3

Verses 1-2. In the light of the deep meditation on the work of the Messiah in the previous psalms there is only One Person that I can trust my soul to. There is only One Person who has shown Himself willing and able to save my soul from sin and death. It is the LORD – 'the LORD strong and mighty, the LORD mighty in battle' (24:8) who sits enthroned at His Father's right hand.

Just as the Father did not allow Christ to be ashamed or defeated by His enemies, so we also have confidence to ask for the same protection and vindication. The Messiah's victory paves the way for the Church's victory. Christ will give to His Bride the same great care and love that He has received from His Father.

The psalms constantly face us with the two stark options that life presents us with. If we put our trust in the resurrected Messiah, the vindicated Saviour, then we will never be let down, never put to shame. However, if we betray the Saviour through unbelief, then there can be no excuse for us and no escape. We will 'be put to shame' as our treachery takes us to Hell.

2. Show me Your ways – verses 4-5

With our trust in *such* a God, who has been vindicated in action, our very first thought is to learn His ways, to find out how to behave like Him. If His ways have led to the right hand of the Father, the Most Holy Place in heaven, then they are ways worth following.

John 14:4-6 cuts to the heart of this when Jesus said...

"You know the way to the place where I am going." Thomas said to him, "Lord, we don't know where you are going, so how can we know the way?" Jesus answered, "*I* am the way and the truth and the life. No one comes to the Father except through *me*."

To learn 'the ways of Christ' is to get to know Christ. He does not have a special technique to teach us. His ways are not mere instructions or theoretical teachings. If we ask for His teaching He will show *Himself* to us through the Scriptures. In His earthly ministry the point of His teaching was always the same – "Follow *ME*! Trust in *ME*!"

Notice the pattern in these verses:

Show me	Your ways
Teach me	Your paths
Guide me	In Your truth

He is my Saviour and my God so I unconditionally and absolutely accept all that He says. 'Let God be true and every man a liar' – Romans 3:4. When His word condemns me, I heartily join in with His condemnation and condemn myself. When His word justifies me through His Cross and Resurrection, then I hold onto that justification whatever condemnations my own heart or the devil throw at me. "My hope is in You all day long".

3. Forgive my iniquity – verses 6-15

In the next section of the psalm, David addresses the problem of his sin. He has already established that the Messiah is His Saviour so that he can approach Him with confidence in this matter.

David begins by pointing back to the "great mercy and love" shown by the LORD in the past. His grace is "from of old". The grace of God in His Messiah is not some short-term 'phase' that He is going through. It is not a 'fad' that He has recently been interested in. This Messianic gospel is from eternity. Before the world began the grace of God was stored up in Jesus Christ for the Church – 2 Timothy 1:9-10 – *"This grace was given us in Christ Jesus before the beginning of time,* but it has now been revealed through the appearing of our Saviour, Christ Jesus, who has destroyed death and has brought life and immortality to light through the gospel." From the creation of the world, the Church trusted in the grace of God in the Promised Messiah who had been promised from the very beginning. [18] When the victory of Christ was achieved at the Cross, it was the fulfilment of all the prophecies that had been given by the Spirit of Christ since Adam and Eve. There is nothing *temporary* about the gospel of Jesus Christ.

David starts from the ancient character of the love of God in His Christ. He wants the LORD to *remember* this ancient love, *but not to remember* David's sins – verse 7. David can remember how bad he was in his youth and he *cannot* forget how he has rebelled against the LORD, but He knows that the Lord *can* forget things.

One of the most powerful and wonderful aspects of the Living God is that He can choose to forget things. When Jeremiah is preaching the gospel in Jeremiah 31:34 he quotes the LORD who says of those who know Him, "I will forgive their wickedness and will remember their sins no more…".

---

[18] Genesis 3:15

We are victims of our memory, unable to forget our sins, often tormented by them long after they have been forgiven in Christ. *The Living God is not limited as we are and is free to forget our sins, to put them infinitely far away – Psalm 103:12.*

While *forgetting David's sins*, David asks that the Lord will *remember David*, not because David isn't so bad after all, but "according to Your love... for *You* are good, O LORD."

The goodness of the LORD sets David off into the next part of the psalm. Precisely because the LORD is good and upright, He instructs sinners in His ways. Sometimes in our sinful views of God, the impression is given that the goodness and righteousness of the LORD is what keeps Him away from us. The truth is the very opposite. It is *because* He is good and upright that He saves us through the gospel. His goodness is shown in His love and patience and kindness and compassion. He is glorified in the salvation of sinners.

Every sinner that humbly (verse 9) calls upon the Messiah will certainly be saved. He shows the humble sinner what is right and shows them how to receive it. The gospel was made specifically for the humble sinner before the world began.

But, isn't the LORD Christ so high and exalted, so full of glory and majesty, so busy with great matters of government beyond our understanding that He can only find a bit of His time and energy for dealing with humble sinners? Surely, most of His business is taken up with other things. NO! verse 10 – "*all* the ways of the LORD are loving and faithful for those who keep the demands of His covenant." The LORD never behaves in any other way towards the humble sinner. The covenant, the gracious gospel, of the LORD governs *all* His ways. Those who shelter in that covenant, that gospel, find Him always loving and gracious, patient and kind.

But, what of these "demands of His covenant"? It sounds very difficult to keep all these "demands". But no! Verse 11 explains. If we ask forgiveness for our sins, even if our sins are many and terrible, simply on the basis of the Name of the LORD, then He will forgive them. His covenant asks nothing of us other than to love and trust His Messiah, seeking in Him and Him alone the forgiveness of our sins.

In verses 12-15 this is explained further. Proverbs 9:10 tells us that "The fear of the LORD is the beginning of wisdom…". This is one of the great themes of Scripture – see Job 28:28; Psalm 111:10; Proverbs 1:7; 2:5; 14:27; 15:33; 16:6; 19:23; 23:17; and Isaiah 33:6. "The fear of the LORD" is the love, trust and worship of the LORD. It is what Christ asks of us if we are to follow Him.

So, David explains why we should respond to the Christ in this way. If we fear Him, He will instruct us in the way that the Lord has for us.

There is a wonderful promise in verse 13. At first we might think that it is strange to be told that we will "inherit the land". If the land spoken of is the land of Israel why would Christians all over the world want to inherit a little bit of land at the end of the Mediterranean?

Well, 'the land' did not just mean a little bit of Middle Eastern geography to the Old Testament saints. For them that land was *a witness* to the whole creation being renewed at the end of the world. Remember what Hebrews 11:8-10; 13-16 says about Abraham, Isaac and Jacob. They lived in tents in the land to show that the physical land was not what they were going to inherit. Their hope was fixed on the City of God on Resurrection Morning. They saw what the land was really all about. It was a token or physical guarantee of the restored creation that the whole church will inherit together at the end of all things.

We see this in the way that Jesus quoted Psalm 37:11. David said that the meek will inherit the land, but Jesus explains what was in David's mind when He says (Matthew 5:5) "Blessed are the meek for they will inherit *the earth*." This is clearly what Psalm 37 means by 'the land' (see Psalm 37:9, 11, 22, 29, 34).

With this great hope before us, the LORD lets us know what He is doing – verse 14. The LORD is not hiding His great plans from us.

He has let us know what He is doing with the whole universe. Such intimacy and privilege means that we never need to look to anybody else (verse 15) for any answers. The LORD alone can save us from our sins and deliver us into that marvellous future in 'the land'.

4. Be gracious to me – verses 16-21

David is revelling in the gospel of the Lord's Christ. His heart and mind are fixed on the ascended Messiah who will restore the whole universe for His Church to live in forever. This gives him tremendous confidence to call out to the Lord in his need.

David's prayers here have a child-like trust about them. He knows that he can pour out his heart to the Lord. The Lord's ways are always loving and faithful to him because he does fear the Lord. In his loneliness, David wants the company of Christ most of all – verse 16. Most of us would ask that the Lord would send us some friends when we are lonely, but because David loves Christ with his whole heart, there is nobody whose friendship he wants more. Christ alone can really soothe the troubles of his heart – verse 17. The way for David to be soothed in his afflictions (verse 18) is for his sins to be taken away. David is always clear about the real issue in life.

If we fear the Lord we need fear nothing else. So, when his enemies are against him, verses 19-21, David looks only to the Lord for safety and refuge. It is not for David to vindicate himself. In Deut. 32:35 the Lord reassures His people that they do not need to fight their own battles against evil enemies- "It is mine to avenge; I will repay. In due time their foot will slip; their day of disaster is near and their doom rushes upon them…".

Of course, what is so striking about this prayer of David is that he has learned how to pray from the prayers of the Messiah. We have seen in Psalm 20 how the Church prays for the future Messiah and in Psalm 22 how Christ calls upon His Father for rescue. Now, David prays in this way for himself. That is the great lesson of the psalms.

The very last verse of the psalm lifts David from the troubles of his own life, with his own persecutions and sin, to the much bigger perspective of the whole Church. "Redeem Israel, O God, from all their troubles!" We should never become so locked into our own situation that we lose sight of our place in the Church, the Bride of Christ. Although Christ deals with our individual situations, He does not deal with us as a huge collection of individuals but as members of His Church. We are saved and protected as members of His Body. Our troubles, our sins are part of the troubles and sins of the whole Church which is washed and protected by Christ.

Further Questions

1. Verse 3 mentions the "treacherous without excuse". Who are these, and why are they without excuse? Surely there must be some people in the world who will be able to provide good excuses for not hoping in the Messiah! Will all those who have not trusted in Jesus be condemned? Or is every single person without excuse? (Romans 1:20 and Colossians 1:23).

2. David describes the Lord's mercy and love as "of old". How old? What does he mean by this when Jesus has not yet been born?

3. What are the "demands of His covenant", verse 4? What have they constantly been for all the different forms of the covenant throughout the Bible?

Daily Readings

Sunday:	Psalm 25
Monday:	Luke 7:36-50
Tuesday:	Psalm 103
Wednesday:	Proverbs chapter 3
Thursday:	Romans 3:9-31
Friday:	Psalm 46
Saturday:	2 Thessalonians chapter 1

BIBLE STUDY 5: PSALM 25

As David considers the great work of his Lord, his heart goes up in praise and he is aware of his own sinfulness before the Lord.

1. How does verse 1 follow on from the previous psalm which speaks of Christ ascending into heaven?

2. How far can we 'adopt' this psalm as our own prayer?

3. Verses 1-3 are very confident in the victory of those who trust the Lord. How do we know that the righteous will not be put to shame? How can this help us endure opposition in our daily lives?

4. How do we learn the ways of the Lord and be guided by Him as in verses 4 & 5? What does this mean in practical terms? (see Psalm 119, verses 1-8 for example)

5. According to verses 6 & 7, what is the amazing thing about the way the Lord forgives our sins? (See also Jeremiah 31:34)

6. We may often feel scared or ashamed to come to the Lord because of His goodness and righteousness. What do verses 8 & 9 have to tell us about that idea?

7. Verses 12-15 talk about the fear of the Lord. What does this actually mean in our Christian lives? (Proverbs 9:10 and John 17:3). What happens to the person who does fear the Lord?

8. How does verse 14 challenge our sinful view of the Lord when we think that He hides His plans from us? What effect must this have in our relationship with Him?

9. David is lonely, full of sinfulness, upset and hated. In verses 16-21, what does he pray for? Why doesn't he just ask for good friends around him?

10. The psalmist has so much confidence in this prayer. How? Should we learn to be like this in our prayers, and if so, how? (Hebrews 4:14-16)

Psalm 27: The Lord Is My Salvation [19]

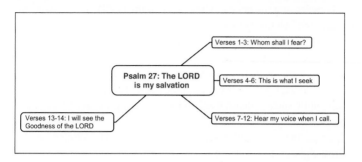

Key Truth: Learning from the sufferings of the Messiah, this psalm teaches us how to trust the LORD in the face of opposition.

Psalm 26 is such a contrast to Psalm 25. In Psalm 25 David lifts his soul up to the ascended Messiah in order for his sins to be forgiven. The whole psalm is focused on Christ dealing with David's sins. However, *whoever is praying Psalm 26 has no sins at all*.

The 'speaker' of this psalm has led "a blameless life" (verse 1 and 11) and can examine every part of their life knowing that no sin can be found there. In fact, they ask the LORD (26:2) to test them to see if even *He* can find something wrong in their heart or mind! This seems to be the same Person who was looking forward to "the great assembly" in Psalm 22. In other words, it is the sinless Messiah Himself.

That is important for the context of the following psalms. Psalm 27 is a cry for vindication and shelter in the day of trouble, ending with confidence that even death will be overcome by resurrection.

---

[19] If you are familiar with Hebrew and the teaching Messianic Jews, you will know that this psalm literally begins with the words: "The LORD is my light and my Yeshua (Jesus)".

Psalm 28 carries forward the same prayer, that the wicked enemies will not drag the Christ into the pit. Psalm 29 is an amazing song acknowledging the ability of 'the voice of the LORD' to deal with the judgement of the Lord – (the judgement of God is symbolised in thunder, mighty waters, breaking of cedars, the lightning, the desert, and most of all, the flood in verse 10). Psalm 30 is such an intimate psalm asking for deliverance from the pit. All this leads up to Psalm 31:1-5. In 31:1-4 there is such a complete and passionate trust in the Lord, until, verse 5, death itself comes. The dying words of Jesus were prophesied in Psalm 31:5 by David – see Luke 23:46. These psalms open up the mind and heart of the Messiah as He suffered on the Cross right up to His death.

If Psalm 26 asserts Christ's innocence, and Psalms 27-30 express His confidence in the Lord to rescue Him from death and His enemies, then Psalm 31 is the concluding prayer in the death of Christ. From Psalm 32 the psalms take on a new direction.

So, in Psalm 27 we are sharing in Christ's own prayer of dependence on His Father. He throws Himself entirely on the LORD as His light and salvation in His troubles. This is where we learn how to depend on the LORD in our own troubles.

This is a master class in prayer from the Master Himself as He prayed to His Father.

None of us experience the level of opposition and suffering that Christ Himself endured, but in all our troubles He is still our model, our pattern. Even in the insults and back-biting of our work and neighbourhood, it is the example of Christ's prayers in these psalms that must control and inspire our own prayers.

1. Whom shall I fear? – verses 1-3

The psalm begins with a clear statement of the Messiah's relationship to His Father. The LORD is His light, salvation and stronghold. It is not that He *gives* light, salvation and a stronghold, but that *He is* those things. The powers of darkness, condemnation and persecution cannot overcome the Lord who *is* light, salvation and a stronghold. There is no need for any fears at all if our security is found only in the LORD. This was Christ's own experience. He could remain so gracious and loving in such terrible opposition because He was not overcome by fear. He knew that He was in His Father's care. So, verse 2, when the evil men and the enemies arrive, they cannot possibly succeed. Even if an army comes against Him (v.3), He will be confident in the LORD.

When we see how graciously Jesus behaved throughout His earthly life when faced with terrible opposition, we might well simply stand back in amazement thinking that it is impossible to behave like He did. However, He has shared His secret with us. If we fear the Lord, then there is no need to fear anyone or anything else. If we are clear that our place in the new creation is absolutely guaranteed by the Lord, then nobody can take away what is ultimately important.

2. This is what I seek – verses 4-6

Only *one thing* is asked of the LORD. We might expect all kinds of things to be asked: physical safety; lots of friends; popularity; material prosperity. However, the one thing that is asked of the Lord is to see the beauty of the Lord where He lives in His temple. Above all else He wants to live in His Father's Presence. If that is certain then all other matters fall into place.

Verse 4 takes us back to Psalm 23:6. No matter what may happen in this life, no matter what suffering and rejection is suffered, if the resurrection hope is certain then all is well. In the day of trouble (verse 5) safety can be found with the Lord. Notice the language:

Keep me safe	In His dwelling
Hide me	In His tabernacle
Set me	Upon a Rock.

The rock upon which He is set is addressed in the very next psalm – Psalm 28:1.

Jesus the Messiah had set His heart and mind on the joy set before Him (Hebrews 12:2). We have seen in Psalm 22:22ff that part of that joy was His fellowship with the Church, but the context for that fellowship is given here. He longs to be in the presence of His Father enjoying the worship of the Church.

This teaches us how to pray. We shouldn't simply pray that the Lord will take away the temporal troubles we are suffering. This is not how Jesus Christ prayed. When we pray to Our Father we must ask for what will give us unshakeable and lasting joy and peace.

Much more valuable than an easy life is that He comforts us with the great hope that we have in Christ. If our hearts and minds are fixed on the joy set before us, just as Christ's were, then we will respond to persecution and suffering in the way that He did.

Do we daily think about the great joy that we will experience on Resurrection Morning? If we do not then it will always seem a vague and mysterious hope that has little impact on our daily living. In the Lord's Promised Messiah we have a certain future of endless joy and wonderful fellowship in the renewed creation, seeing the Father's face. Only a future so marvellous can outweigh the troubles we may face in this life.

3. Hear my voice when I call – verses 7-12

Again we are brought back to the *one thing*. Nothing in life matters if we have the comfort of the Lord. If He listens to us, then we can bear being ignored or opposed by others. Christ cried out to His Father and nothing mattered to Him if He had His Father's attention. Hebrews 5:7 – "During the days of Jesus' life on earth, He offered up prayers and petitions with loud cries and tears to the One who could save Him from death, and He was heard because of His reverent submission."

Verse 8 is striking. The desire of His heart was to seek the face of the Lord. It was the *one thing* that He couldn't ignore. The thought of Him turning His face away (verse 9) is too terrible. "Do not reject or forsake me, O God my Saviour". When we remember the desolate cry of Psalm 22, this prayer is so deep. If He prayed these words on the Cross, it shows that the words of Psalm 22:1 were not the end of His prayers, but merely the beginning. He continued to call out to His Father, seeking His face, asking for His mercy. He could not bear to be forsaken by His Father.

In verse 10 even one of the worst rejections of all is contemplated. What if my own mother and father completely rejected me? How could I possibly cope with that? Surely it is impossible for anyone to survive such rejection? Yet, the psalm tells us that the acceptance of the Lord will outweigh even such rejection.

So, verse 11, it is the ways of the Lord that must be learned. If knowing Him can bring us through the most severe suffering and rejection, then we must turn to Him alone to lead us on the straight path.

We see just how verse 12 happened in Jesus' own trial. His enemies made plans to get Him and brought false witnesses against Him – Mark 14:55-59. When such things happen to us, we must follow this example of Christ. Instead of trying to vindicate ourselves, we must turn to our heavenly Father for our vindication. His opinion about us far outweighs all others.

4. I will see the goodness of the Lord – verses 13-14

In the middle of all this turmoil the faith of Christ remains rock-solid. Whatever the threats of His enemies, however many lies were told about Him, whatever violence was brought against Him, yet He knew that He would be vindicated in the Resurrection. He knew that He would see the goodness of the Lord in the land of the living. When we remember the terrible rejection He experienced in Psalm 22, this certain hope is so strong.

The psalm ends with the essential point – "wait for the Lord". If we listen to the lies of sinful humanity we will lose our direction. Our hope and peace will be taken away. If we focus on our enemies then we will start to fear them and give in to them. However, if we follow the example of the Messiah, then we will 'wait for the Lord'. While He was hanging on the Cross it must have been so hard to trust that everything was in the hands of the Father, that He would receive such a resounding vindication so soon after His death in the resurrection. However, He was able to be strong because He knew that the Lord would not let Him down.

This psalm is such an encouragement to us. The Lord will never let us down. Whatever rejection we suffer, He will never forsake us. If we 'wait for the Lord' and 'seek His face' we will never be disappointed.

Further Questions

1. What is the dwelling and tabernacle spoken of in verse 5? Where else in the Bible do we read of this?

2. For some people suffering makes them bitter and full of resentment towards the Living God. For other people suffering refines them and brings them nearer to the Lord. For some, suffering is the argument against God, for others it is the place where God is truly known. What divides the world in this way? (1 Peter 1: 6-9).

3. Karl Marx criticised religion for being a way of keeping people suppressed by telling them about 'pie in the sky when you die' rather than essential food right now. If we think about our resurrection hope every day will we become less loving to the problems of hunger, poverty and injustice?

Daily Readings

Sunday: Psalm 27

Monday: Psalm 28 & 29

Tuesday: John chapter 3

Wednesday: Isaiah chapter 55

Thursday: 1 Timothy 2:1-13

Friday: Revelation chapter 22

Saturday: Psalm 30 & 31

BIBLE STUDY 6: PSALM 27

The promised Messiah experienced the worst hatred, rejection, opposition and death, and He suffered it all from the people He lovingly created. Nevertheless in this prayer He teaches us how to pray and trust in the Father for salvation.

1. Why is it significant that the Lord does not merely give us light, salvation and stronghold in verses 1 & 2? How do we get these things?

2. What does the Messiah teach us about opposition and persecution in this psalm? What do we need to remember to help us deal with such attacks?

3. What is the secret of not being afraid of anyone?

4. If you could ask the Father for one thing (as verse 4), what would your desire be? Why did Jesus ask for this thing?

5. What is the rock spoken of in verse 5? (Psalm 28:1)

6. When we are suffering pain or persecution, should our first reaction be to pray for it to be taken away? If not, why not?

7. What is it that enables Christ to persevere? What occupies His thoughts in verses 4-6?

8. In verses 7-10, what thing is feared most? What did happen on the Cross?

9. How did verse 12 happen to the Messiah?

10. What does it mean to "wait on the LORD" (verse 14)? How do we do this in our walk with Him?